T0113713

Pride Aside & Other Poems

Bill F. Ndi

Langaa Research & Publishing CIG
Mankon, Bamenda

Publisher:

Langaa RPCIG
Langaa Research & Publishing Common Initiative Group
P.O. Box 902 Mankon
Bamenda
North West Region
Cameroon
Langaagrp@gmail.com
www.langaa-rpcig.net

Distributed in and outside N. America by African Books Collective
orders@africanbookscollective.com
www.africanbookscollective.com

ISBN: 9956-763-61-6

DISCLAIMER
All views expressed in this publication are those of the author and do
not necessarily reflect the views of Langaa RPCIG.

Table of Contents

Pride Aside..1

My Love and I.......................................2

For musing on *Up from Slavery*........................ 6

Wind Song.. 8

Sing their Deceit.................................... 9

Eye and I.. 10

Slaughterhouse....................................... 11

Blind to the Lamp................................... 13

Deafening Silence................................... 14

April Hails Fools................................... 15

Swimming to Safety.................................. 16

In this Game.. 17

The Color of my Dolor............................... 18

Apostate.. 19

Our Union Spring.................................... 20

The Seeds of Demos.................................. 23

PPP..24

The Man and His Minions............................. 25

how we fly...26

TiLi (Take it/Leave it)............................. 27

On the Pitch.. 28

My Humble Pie....................................... 29

Ready... 30

Give no Reason......................................32

Keep Watch.. 33

Upholsterer's Footrest..............................34

Dark Days... 35

The Foe's Game......................................36

Of Pride and Effacement............................. 37

The Flag to Fly..38

Sing Blackness...39

Pride's Dwelling Place....................................40

My Incontrovertible Choice...........................41

The Foe's Flash..42

Light on My Stance.......................................43

Dreamer in Trance..44

Of Little and Big Things...............................45

My Sentinel vs. the Blower...........................47

Put it off...48

Dejected Delight...49

Of Grass and Class.......................................50

Gentle knocks...51

Not Fallen...52

Cling on..53

Hoody Hoodlums..54

Laced Pavements..55

Bandless Music...56

This Gilded Smile...57

Of Humiliation, not Simulation...................58

Wisdom at Eighteen.....................................59

By His Might...60

My Choice to Climb Down...........................61

Why Hurry? 62

Forget Not...63

An Embrace with Failure..............................64

Hardened Nutshell..65

Bloom in the Tomb.......................................66

Stainless Reflection.......................................67

The Stride of Pride..68

Bamboo Life Raft...69

Gilded Crown of Demise...............................70

Man's Rubbisher.....................................71

Pride Made Outfits................................72

Childhood Humbleness............................73

Of Skunks and Pride...............................74

Lilliputian's Brobdingnagian Pride..............75

Gift from the Spook................................76

Above the Fray.....................................77

Long-legged Humbleness........................78

Not for the Proud..................................79

My World...80

What and Where to Plant........................81

Of Glut and Pride.................................82

Treasure Slave.....................................83

Thieving Royals....................................84

The Sparkles of Pride.............................85

The Gloom of Meekness.........................86

The Loser Wins....................................87

Of Stocks and Bridges............................88

The Bait I won't Take.............................89

Pride Aside

I have had my shoulders wet with tears
I would they were of joys made not fears
Today, lost in thoughts, I was caught
Deep down under where a distraught
Soul my shoulders sought with a well
Of lachrymal flow swollen to tell
The unsure hope of the unborn
That her life's of misery adorn.
My shoulder saw not her whiteness
Nor did her eyes see my blackness
In our color sensitive world
Where colorlessness is no word
And colors birth utter bleakness
Of Man's dignity and meanness.

My Love and I

Silence!
Oh!
Silence!
How I am in love with your music!
You strike the hidden chord and cure the sick
The sick who in their ignorance find bliss
Bliss with the snake, out of sight, not its hiss
Silence!
Oh!
Silence!
When in my sleep you roar like thunder,
You grace my night with deep slumber
And invite the flower to come color
My vision and chase away dolor!
Silence!
Oh!
Silence!
I would run amok for missing you
'Coz in this world you're unique, not two
For though I love pairs you'd better be
Single and have my bonnet bee free!
Silence!
Oh!
Silence!
With you by me, visitation comes
Home to keep me in such topmost forms
To still trees in the grip of a tempest
Oh! My love, how with you I know rest!
Silence!
Oh!

Silence!
You surprise me not with your caress
For every resting soul you impress
Upon the rule of thumb to seal mouths
And never bother any with pouts.
Silence!
Oh!
Silence!
You by me, I pick pen and paper
To spice eyes and ears like hot pepper
And clear sight and further make hearing
Clearer without any red herring.
Silence!
Oh!
Silence!
Without you, how restive will life be?
You fill my cup full with sweet honey
Enough of which I would never have
And will still crave your charm in my grave
Silence!
Oh!
Silence!
Let me stop this litany and make
Not of you bare noise for its own sake
For yours is music played without sound
Nor words and assures one safe and sound
Silence!
Oh!
Silence!
There again, you come to make me see
This world translated into a sea
In which swims not losses but gains

Far away from all that which brings pains.
Silence!
Oh!
Silence!
In this sea, I'd fish to fill a creel
In which both big and small fish
Shall make thundery stomachs to sit still
And watery mouths to smack of your dish:
Silence!
Oh!
Silence!
When in my sleep you translate the world
Into splendors without any word,
A kiss from Morpheus makes you my star
Crossed lover no rendition would mar
Silence!
Oh!
Silence!
Pushed to the wall with noise of treachery
I voice not a word to break your heart
For our tacit pact makes me diehard
With power entombed in your mystery;
Silence!
Oh!
Silence!
Yours is mystery to the world. Not me!
For, as your lover, I would not leave
You nor let fall off our tree a leaf
That'd whisper in Fall you set me free!
Silence!
Oh!
Silence!

In you silence, sweet silence, you muse
In my thirsty ears love songs I'd die
For, were I to tell the world a lie
You quench not my thirst that'll be abuse
Silence!
Oh!
Silence!
You are that just drop of honey, sweet
Honey and would catch a zillion flies;
Feat which an ocean of gall can't rise
Above for your sweetness is my treat
Silence!   Oh!   Silence!

For musing on *Up From Slavery*

I once wore the label Booker T.
And no more than heard of Tuskegee
Where I, now, am and would I were hom
Sweet home, far from their bittersweet home
Alaban

Of yesteryears' memory when sun's blade
Slashed forebears in the grip of white trade
Which left my kind a load they're not men
With me
Caught in seeking what they could have meant
Stowing away beautiful black brains
From our trees' city of pouring rains
With nature's bestowal of the reins
To our stock to frame this resistance
That blazes our trail of persistence
Passion, patience, and perseverance
As spur and drive to keep us afloat
And have no need for oars and a boat
Or better still dread not to go down
The abyss they prepared us for dawn.
Then
And
Only
Then
Shall I
Shall Booker T,
Shall You,
And shall we all smile
Back at

Victory

Who shall drum its music all alone
In voiceless hearts of ours like a drone
Combing the horizon with a smile
To leave awondering any senile.

Wind Song

Wending my way down the forest
     I found a tree
     On which tree
I'd backed up to steal some rest
Whereon the leaves let the wind
To sing in my ears such kind
Words that drive home in a drone
The love this tree alone
           For centuries
     In my reveries
Drummed in hope the clay footed
Washed their clayey feet of fetid
Rank to breathe th'oxygen the tree
Doth release for man with no fee.

02/08/2015

Sing their Deceit

Having chimed such tunes no one dances to
Will you let me Lord, like the wind blow through
The pine trees to let whispers flood deaf ears
And move them; hearts, souls, and feet without fears
To stomp the grounds of perfidy acclaimed
By the empire's to have my kind maimed
And your leafy branch letting my wind
Fondles and takes her out of a bind?
My heart will not stop beating as
You and only You are worth this class
To groom souls who'd never die
And above perfidy fly
With need to look up to You
Alpha and Omega never two!

2/08-10/2015

Eye and I

Science, tell me not what ye know not
As you strive to crack your hard nut
Let me sip this fluid that shapes life
Without need for a carving knife
That has carved and deformed mankind,
De-named, and rechristened my kind
Chattel with no history to tell
Like that tall tale history would sell
 To the world not my sweet story
Which to tell one needs not worry
And need not slave to justify
As you toil to have your lie fly
'Coz I'm in love with the kernel
You get from the hard nut you shell.

Slaughterhouse

I walked down our childhood lane
My withering flowers craving moisture
Brought me to children scared not of mane
Nor lionman's readiness with a cane
To thrash their butt for daring to dream
They themselves were the cream de la cream

These children,
Those of yore,
As well as
Those to come
Have always
Visitation had
Come and dress them
For professions
That, in their dreams
Flower and writhe not
With pain driven
Home from a pride
They've pushed aside…

How these children like their robes!
How those children loved their white scrubs!
And those to come in their pinafore locked!
With all showing molar to molar!
Whence comes the lionman with his old mortar
With which he'd pound nursery dreams tucked

In the hearts of morning birds soaring
The sky with no thought their death knows no mourning!

02/23/2015

Blind to the Lamp

See and call our congregations
That of fools, unfit to move motions
Remain blind to the lamb that's our strength
All along on whom victory, at length,
Shall be wrapped and flown on a tall mast.
In the wind it flaps and is steadfast
In sending us motions which by you
Is the preserve of only a few
. Of whom our kind is not but their scum
And we continue to beat our drum
For ears that hear and feet that can dance
As the thrill comes along in a trance;
As Blake beholds, in the valley's wild,
Our Savior on the cloud as a child.

03/20-21/2015

Deafening Silence

I bounced round their world in feats
And in every city
And each of their streets
Silence was rowdy
Silent feasts over the scum
Preempting this storm
Far from those in quest of petrol
Under cover of desert storm
With ilk of misery enraged with no dessert
To shake off this lot heaped
And contorted to blur their trail
And blind black memory with a wag of the tail;
Memory of a glorious past
'Coz imposed misery shan't last.

05/01/2015

April Hails Fools

Here comes April to give me a fool's treat
As seasons roll in and out I won't cheat
The great God's design to make new dust mold
In which He breathes in life that can't be sold
But for pigmenting my mold, my kind
Of such deprived would I were in a bind
Bundled from sea to sea and passed from hand
To hand to end up with my hat in hand
My pride they would I swallowed and sit still
Still I refuse to be hailed fool at will
One that's so far remote from the divine
Whose desire never was to see me pine
But eye me joy to savor His mercy
And grace in abundance far from their sea.

April-May 2015

Swimming to Safety

Of spikes and thorns the sea's been made for me
One through which I would swim to safety
Shielded by Him whose crown of the same make
On anguish, misery, and glitch hits the break
Turning all tears of pain to those of gain
For all who to Him give their hearts not brain,
Citadel wherefrom blames rock their way out
In vain attempt to trick a heart to pout
And polish the foe's face with a lean grin
The like of one who's had a shot of gin
My heart I harden to avoid a fall
For it is the only way to stand tall
Above those shooting for material things
To pride themselves in lording over rings.

May 3rd 2015

In This Game

In this game may divine plan be to me
Wedded in true holy matrimony
I see with wings on a post flapping high
And pushing away rain clouds from the sky
As the wind brings forth tidings to our cast
Here on borrowed time soon to be our past
Not divine will which was, is and will be
The robe whose basket is full of honey
A taste of which we'll never have enough
As we game, bask, and relax by the trough
For the hand we pick is by grace handed
For which reason I'd not be divided
Running after two hare at the same time
For all my ear hears is His game plan's chime.

The Color of my Dolor

Your inner heart darker than the color
The color of my skin, source of dolor
You inflict on me and claim yours a shine
I need follow to outshine the moonshine
In your brain that steals the slightest prospect
You need to heed the voice within 'n respect
Not me but He who wrought both you and me
And assigned my land far across the sea
From yours such that you drag me not so low
To convert my love into an arrow
In rage and out of anger far from my
Tea, mercy I delight to sip and fly
Above this pain that gloss of yours doth breathe
To bring down my kind beneath a wreath.

5/19/2015

Apostate,

Go tell the potentate
I don't want him dead
As he wants me dead
For I won't embrace his hate

For a state that my love blooms
For and refuses to die
For him to smirk at my cry
For having posed his glooms grooms

For me to reach my hand to
Dress with the comb of a cox
For him to see himself fox
Forgetting I remain true

To the Book by a Ruler
That guides my path like ruler.

June-July 2015

Our Union Spring

Crimson red blood underneath black skin
Crimson red blood underneath blond skin
Crimson red blood underneath blue skin
Crimson red blood underneath brown skin
Crimson red blood underneath dark skin
Crimson red blood underneath pale skin
Crimson red blood underneath pink skin
Crimson red blood underneath red skin
Crimson red blood underneath thick skin
Crimson red blood underneath thin skin
Crimson red blood underneath white skin
Crimson red blood beneath yellow skin

You alone underneath every skin

Make of all mankind a wholesome kin
Most of whom seem, in their caprice, blind
And would humanness by skin
Color that to the colorless bind

And defined pigmented who is not
For fine arts know not them as colored
And such comes from one who's lost a knot
And like Sisyphus not being bored

Rolling uphill a stone that won't stay
But bent on making his kind object
Reduced to subject of the abject
On the fringes with no way to play

Crimson red blood like an hour glass shows
The quintessence which is never seen
Crimson red blood from Christ washes sin
And does not prey on us as would crows.

Crimson red blood alone unearth dearth
By white snow masqueraded under
And buried abysmally like death
Struck, shattered, and shredded by thunder.

Crimson red blood brighten red badges
Crane named of courage only one man
I know carried to rid us of grudges
That would have paved the way to be wan

Crimson red blood you give strength to stay
Away from the moil of diurnal toil
Which graces our canvas with its soil
And leaves us with needful hearts to pray.

Crimson red blood without which we're damned!
He who doubts needs bring home a life void
Of Crimson red blood that be not damned
And would still sit up and not be destroyed.

Crimson red blood on the shroud shows Black!
That tells the tale of suffering untold
Meted on those forced into their arc
Not by floods pushed to cross but by gold.

Crimson red blood on which my trust stand
In my ears whisper the need for me

To shout their gold statues stand on sand
And from bondage would not set them free

Crimson red blood intone in my ears
Chants that would push to the dancing floor
Bodies that would quiver without fears
And would mundane vanity deplore.

Crimson Red Blood you cleanse with your grace
And spare the prideful who asserts might
In blind leap to embrace his disgrace
'Coz you doubt not might is yours by right.

For in your slow flow you wax me strong,
Rubbing like a sea sand grain a pearl
Whose sheen of a cherub little girl
Summons my heart to beat like a gong

The beat of which brings me to your court
Where like a drifter in the desert
By an oasis need no dessert
But thirst quenching as it is so hot.

The Seeds of Demos

They rain such seeds of democrat y
Everywhere and anywhere without
Care they'd come by infertility
Swimsuit in a cesspool of draught

And with their spell they would they inject
Life into our dead horse long interred
Following tradition and respect
With which heroic horses are transferred

To the land of no worries away
From the chimeras here sold to us
With the sold goal to empty our purse
In their chaos brought from faraway

With such wisdom that cast a lowly
Look at ours for riding on gently.

PPP

It pricked once, twice, and pricked and pricked and pricked
The poets who pointed to that which had pricked
The masses in their slumber and blind trust
For a caretaker busy raising dust
With which he would blind them as they awake
To this new thorn bloom they trusted a snake
And of the poets made such clowns for standing
Their ground and tempting the sovereign swindling
Behind the raised particles he himself
Had blown with hot air to end the poets' delve
And left paint strokes of poet's as woe bringer
Whose only desire as harbinger
Is to herald misery for the masses
Far from political preaching praxis.

The Man and His Minions

How can one man a dominion make of millions?
Would any dare say he would without his minions?
And where else would these lackeys elect home if not
Amongst those crying how they've been reduced to naught?
To question the obvious is to unbundle pride
Sieve and shift and bring to light those who stand astride
And would with both sides of their mouth blow hot and cold
As if for our freedom we were after the gold
After which dominion maker poisons grassroots
And for which my pen bleeds the crimson of beetroots
That in the years of yore stood in lieu of sugar
The accumulation of which blacken like tar
The vigor of the sickening sweet toothed blind
Minions whose forethoughts grow stomach and teeth to grind.

how we fly

without a pie
keen on
your heart beat

for which i
would gun
not to bleed

but to hug
with love
from deep down

without fog
just love
that won't drown

neither you
nor i
we'd both soar

show new hue
up high
with no roar
in our world
in which
you and i

without word
on switch
as we fly

fly on heart
towards

your true love

dodge the dart
and swords'
strikes in drove

after you
to slay
this true goal

that makes you
this day
make me whole

only in
our world
would we know

peace within
impearled
by juno.

TiLi (Take it/Leave it)

Life's not a scorpion that stings without cause
But like a river, it charts one a course
Take it or leave it, its course 'twill follow
With no aim at bringing your spirit low
As its excitement distend one's members
The memory of which flashes ambers
To brighten the bleak gloom in the present
And give no one reason for this recent
Spate of aches of John Osborn's resonance
Where life as a couple should spell romance.
With that buried? One must embrace that which
Brings forth the sweet savoring memories of yore
With soothing whispers to translate a lore
In which affection doth entomb the glitch.

On the Pitch

hold two with same wish
bind them with one stitch
let no one tell you
a tale of an ewe
lost in the mountain
when the shepherd went
behind his small tent
with hope a fountain
would his thirst smother
as would a mother
a child's with honey sweet
milk from mammary sweet
nipples with trickle
children's mouths tickle.

My Humble Pie

My pie is humble
I must be able
To eat it without
Dreams it were a trout
For the fish I have
To fry need not have
Bones to stick in
In the throat of man
Who finds delight in
The light that his tan
Gloss to spark the rage
Of foes who in him
See only a scheme
To take center stage.

Ready

Tell me why I need not keep it low
I would let you know why those cows low
For the humps they carry cry and tell
The burden heaped on me is a stele
Which I need not bother to carry
Till the day I turn down all merry
Making and task them to see me off
Not for I judged their love not enough
But 'coz of joy to end a journey
Laden with toil to amass money;
Money who's no man's friend for it comes
And goes as would the tides without qualms
And were I to worry nil will change
As the money itself is called change.

Over the Pit

Shades and hues we see or paint
Would change nothing from the taint
Pride and arrogance bought us
Festering our wounds with pus
And to this day we must sit
And rethink over the pit
We dug for ourselves with pride
Bent on being our new bride
Who'd not settle for divorce
But would keep us loose by force
In shit storm our pride left out
Would have ripened our bailout
We now need to learn to peel
Off and let fall to be steel.

Give no Reason

Learn not to blacken your black black
As none wants to see you on track
So they'd jump on the occasion
To allot out of proportion
Cruelty to your lot in dire
Need to burn despair with fire
And bury her ashes six feet
Under the ground you stomp with feet
For you must deflate the bubble
In which you entreat your trouble
With a can of black paint in hand
And brush strokes that stain the grand stand
On which your path to forge ahead
Lies and all you need is a head

Keep watch

Your eyes must be wide open to see
Mainly for you're forced across the sea
And stripped naked to the bone under
The blazing sun of southern cotton
Fields wherein with a hard heart of stone
God's blessed unions were put asunder
With claims of dominion over you
And you they told you were from you
But an object of theirs to abuse
And abuse they did abuse and use
You and would have your kings they call chiefs
Dressed in the garment of their mischief
As you bury your head underneath
The quest for scrap trinkets from the heath.

Upholsterer's Footrest

When I make myself carpet and footstool,
My upholsterer's footrest, I found
Rest of body, mind, and soul that a fool
Would make an uphill task far from the ground
On which to stand away from the quicksand
Drifting sinker away from the hard rock
On which needs stand the chip of the old block
To be the décor that adorns this brand
Whose flag flaps and flies sky high far above
The stand on which worldly wise egos rove
And drag down that which makes up human quest
On earth where the one needful thing is rest
That the haughty only find in their grave
Once they've pawned away their lives as the brave.

9/6/2015

Dark Days

In the haze of a dark cloud
I stoop low and am steel proud
Above was such a Father
So close he won't go farther
Afield to leave my soul low
And let me to be that child
Marooned and standing beguiled
As the glass its sand grain loses
For the smoothness that glosses
Her comes through a fiery glow
From a pipe a blower blows
Giving her shape, form, and way
Just the way His light follows
And shines my steps all the way.

1/29/2015

The Foe's Game

The wiles, guiles, and ruses of the foe
Would hold me down pounding on my toe
Feeding me the food of foolish pride
Thinking not I will know 'tis a trite
Whose span lasts only a short season;
Bait I won't take and commit treason
For I know where my allegiance lies
And that is far away from the lies
Sold to many a man hankering for
Earthly fame headed for a Sulphur
Pit forever flaming with the rage
Of an irate angel in a cage
Deprived of the wherewithal to pull
A stunt on one of his trusting fool.

9/7/15

Of Pride and Effacement

Triple on you the thick layers of pride
And you'd find it wouldn't be a fun ride
Like coating yourself with humility
Like the deliverer on his donkey
Towards the city wherein resides 'peace'
Bringing with him a just message of Peace.
I've tried your garment of deadly sin
And all it did was to prick like a pin
Piercing an aching heart by then full
With filth that with all the knowledge from school
None would ever come close to cleansing clean
Not even when such would with facts demean
And spite Him that fashions the universe
In which such ilk, in haste, end in a hearse.

9/10/2015

The Flag to Fly

Fly the flag of the haughty and bawdy
You'd end up in a crowd that is rowdy
And won't make sense of that cacophony
You have chosen over this euphony
For the choices made never were the fruit
Of a gamble nor song from a strange flute
But conscientious toil with consequences
And no excuse of coincidences
Fly the flag you would, plough your thoughts for shoots
Not that which will lead you to hearing hoots
From winged messengers of the underworld
Whose overlord's all fangs, ropey and curled
Up with readiness to envenom fools
With pride they'd be saved by knowledge from schools.

9/10/15

Sing Blackness

Sing blackness! Sing not in the weird white world
This song that doth my soul caress and smelt
Its magma laden with burns of hate felt
When the chains of hate on forebears were hurled
And today the same would you mute their crimes
For by the way, then and now, blacks and grimes
Are none but two headed dragons they'd kill
For pleasure and have you, blackness sit still
But I would you sang to them that one song
Which swells in your bosom and proves them wrong
For making our kind lesser of the stock
We're all made of and would of our history
Reduce to nothingness; end of story,
For, by them, we excel as laughing stock.

09/11/2015

Pride's Dwelling Place

My pride dwells not by the things of this world
But resting the feet of my manager
Not that on earth who works as a monger
Mongering material trinkets he would meld

At the expense of the weak and lamblike
Whom nature has blessed with strength not to harm
A life but pasture to ornate our farm
On which mundane bosses prey vampire-like.

I glory with the Lamb for He is strength
And rather I were His feed made to dwell
In Him where repose I would find not hell
Or have my life commute an endless length

I won't quest Blake's enthrallment by the lamb
Who may shake well and still outshines a lamp.

09/14/2015

My Incontrovertible Choice

Warm yourself up to dependence with pride.
I'll efface myself to freedom with stride.
Strive to soar above all like an eagle.
I would strive to be a 'musing beagle.
Beam bright with joy to see my kind in plight.
I'd show you that my delight dwells in flight.
Fly your flag of disgrace with its bling bling.
I would hoist that of Peace His mercies bring.
Ephemerality is your forte.
The alpha and omega my main stay.
Onto Him I cling and would not let go.
Such is the act you'd never understand.
And He's my choice on whom to build; not sand
On which you thrust your hope for wind to blow!

09/15/2015

The Foe's Flash

Pride won't burden and blind me to the truth
And drop me where I'm bawdy and uncouth.
Restrain, truth teaches me, would preserve me
From the foe who'd sting to outdo the bee.

Truth teaches me I should love and not hate
Then spend time crying when it is too late
To open my heart to the castaway
Sacred Heart that stands for the only way.

The foe flashes pride and earthly glory
With lies that death is the end of story.

Yet, my immaterial self tells a tale
Only the physic would one day be stale
Without smiles and anything to divide.
Why won't I unburden myself of pride?

09/16/2015

Light on My Stance

Unsound is your discarded disaster
Pride with which you garb yourself as master.
I'd rather be this subaltern who knows
When and where to poke his officious nose
And be lifted high up by the Master
Of the universe who'd your dreams shatter
Leaving your snobbery in bits and pieces.
Like a glass made of sand, why won't you break
When you refuse the blower's hand to take
A leap for the foe who leaves no traces
Of the once upon a time arrogance
That was in and on you to take delight
And crush and slay my kind as you would mite
And today, the Master brightens my stance.

09/17/2015

Dreamer in Trance

In my trance I would not be proud and blind.
I'm in one to forge ahead not behind.
Focused on 'n humble in my way within
Where voice and light stream and bathe me therein
I do swim with my head above the ground
Though buried in the mire of their sound
And fury aimed at drowning the dreamer
In his reverie swimming higher and higher
And leaving the arrogant in their dark night
Choice they have made in hope to find light
At the end of the tunnel which tunnel
Gulps their hopes without spill through a funnel
Squeezing them down its neck devoid of strain
The crush in which channel they taste my pain.

09/22-23/2015

Of Little and Big Things

One million times I bent over
Penny, penny one million times
Produced ten thousand dollar bills
Which I pulled out and was smiled at
To bury the woes of stooping
Low the numerous times I did
I bent over one million times
Each time I stood with a penny
With a penny I raised my head
With a smile and was made fun of
With gawky laughs heard in the state
In hope my meekness lay in state
Yet, all would they caressed the gold
And none would soil his hands for it.

Beneath the dumpster sits the mine
And to touch this ore, one must stoop
As would Stoppard to triumph over
Than be a Tom waiting to see
Before upholding scraps cover
Precious metals worth dirty hands
Dirty hands that could always be
Washed clean and cleaner by such metal
In a world whereby trinkets cloud
Thoughts and choke the inner bright light
That guides towards the little things

As if to say we need recall
We were not always tall but small
For, stowed little things grow big things.

09/25/2015

My Sentinel vs. the Blower

That hot, hot air blown for excellence
Rather fans but flames whose quintessence
Emanates patchiness inside out
Though such hot air tries to mask all doubt,
She falls at my gate where stands the keen
Sentinel unwilling to be weaned
Of his fondness to smell from afar
The glimmer of that kind of fake star
Enticing only the ensnared fools
Who embrace knowledge as bought from schools
And would turn schools to money machine
For in that sphere money is their engine.
Round the clock, my sentinel keeps watch
And denies his garb be left a scratch.

09/26/2015

Put it Off

Don't you see the parasite to delouse?
Pride which rides on one should in him arouse
The desire to rid himself of such pest
Which destroys and will not let him find rest
For it is the burden with which the heart
Is laden and will be, by such a dart,
Punctured; were one not to humble himself
Low and removed from the bedeviled elf.
Low at the bosom of humility
Lie peace, love, and hope in security
As the deloused is slain and put to rest
From which nadir it won't ramp up the crest
To derail the straight thoughts a positive
Mind hugs against that which is destructive.

10/03/2015

Dejected Delight

You bruised, battered, and abuse me mindless
Of Him that cut me to be His likeness
And I blame you not for the fiend, your drive
Of all knowledge and wisdom doth deprive
You to the point you are covered with dough
Not to see that which you delight to show
Nor will you ever come back here after
You have been butted to the hereafter
Far from your dream of crushing mine before
It cuts through the skyline; that you've made lore
Blind a fate awaits your senselessness
That drives you and your ilk to be ruthless
In life that comes to an end as you die
Deprived of the gladness to see me cry!

10/02-03/2015

Of Grass and Class

The swollen balloons that you are are blind;
Too blind to know the deflated balloon
Needs not be told that which made him to swoon
When it was bloated and thinking all fine.

Underneath, I lie low on the river
Floor and form the bed rock without which rock
The cornerstone, once the rejected block,
Would have, with ease, been swept by the water.

Let out some of the airs from your thin skin
And you would be at peace with all your kin
And I'd have a lesson to learn from you

As I need not be the one to teach you
Being a mere root of a common grass
You cut for fodder for those without class.

10/05/2015

Gentle knocks

"Time will tell"
Water told the hardened rock
"What will time tell?
Questioned the hardened rock.

My ears drank with mirth
This dialogue from birth
Without knowing what
I would make of that.

I saw time come and go
And kept its pace slow
And this made me eager
To see water winner.

Gently water made gain
Waring rock grain by grain.

10/05/2015

Not Fallen

At sunrise I step onto the sidewalk
To follow the trail blazed not for the balk
But for me by the unique righteous hand
That fashions this splendor on which I stand
In meek readiness not to go astray
With knowledge the foe's eyes are on the prey
For which he takes me; forgetting I'm down
To fear neither fall nor his ugly frown
I am down; not fallen and never will
Though the foe would spend time wishing me ill
Thinking not I am walled in by His might
With which I have been blessed as a birth right
And all I need is humiliate myself
To throw off the rails that mistrustful elf.

10/08/2015

Cling on....

I clench to my coxcomb of fool given
By the proud whose pride stinks of putrid rank
Which he sets aside and would want to rank
Me the lowest of low beneath heaven.

I assume my role of a fool on stage
And, this, by choice with no crime seen in it
For were that my lot, I'd cling onto it
And catch eyes as would words on the right page

For words that sit not where they ought to be
Would hasten clouded judgment with their sting
And produce nothing sweet as would a bee
Whose honey droplets flies, to their trap, bring

As I'd rather be this fool than smell rank
And would even let proud pride call me crank.

10/15/15

53

Hoody Hoodlums

He blended me with everything color
Not for you to come and give me dolor
Under the hood with claims the Almighty
Is Arian who'd wish my kind in misery
For his light is not flame touched by human
Hands which should be stretched to place a demand
And not to torch that which the Creator
Shows his mercy upon and would restore
To prove your ghostly garb of false purity
Is not white but depleted honesty
Whitewashed to entrap the absent-minded
With tall tales of how He had intended
His world divided which is not the case
With His people who form One human race.

10/18/15

Laced Pavements

You may maim all rights with arrogant pride;
One you take for a right to heap a plight
Upon those lives you punctuate with fright
And take their groans, moans, and cries for a ride
In your park wherein miseries lace pavements
With your struggle to prove yourself worthy
Of worthlessness that refracts unhealthy
Mind frames framed for underdevelopments
Yet, groans, moans, and cries wrap with envelops
The underdevelopments you yearn for
And would they marked an end to your lore
With your pride buried to let grow new crops
We crave to eat, our humble pie not cake,
And with delectation that we'd not fake!

10/20/2015

Bandless Music

I have travelled roads with that included;
It lay wasted like a python stuffed
With its meal. Quite a sorry sight to see!
For the life in that snaky road had left
And snapped my mouth ajar its journey ends
With lifeless air the conceited won't want
To breathe for they are with their own airs filled
Knowing not a pin drop on a balloon
Would inflame one like an incensed baboon
Raging and banging its head on a tree.
On that benumbed road my drumming heart beat
Boom! Boom! Boom! One with a lamb on bare street
Chills rushed down my spine, my hair stood on strands,
And my heart played sweet music without bands.

10/22/15

This Gilded Smile

Long after my heart played its sweet music
Without bands I revisited basic
Realities never to question why
Here on earth the humble have to be shy.
My eyes have feasted on those full of pride
Heralding theirs before their heavy fall
Where my kind in docile keenness stood tall
Ushering me to where I must abide.
Keeping my profile at its nadir, I
Pick not the crumbs but the finest gold dust
To gild the smile they had wished were a cry
From the anguish stricken they hoped would rust.
The sheen of such smile, now the proverbial
Drop of honey takes more flies in its phial.

10/23/2015

Of Humiliation, not Simulation

Having donned this hat of silence, I listen
With utmost attention to the noise pride
Makes in hope he'd take my world for a ride
With mere jangling from his empty basin
Whose cacophony ensures no import
Aimed at swaying multitudes to despair
And abandoning them in disrepair
As they wake up speechless in a strange port.
Yet, ours as ears propel waves to the brain
And none of which waves is let down the drain
For the donned hat of silence breaks the waves
And hedges in all who would humiliate
Themselves and follow, and not simulate
Worldly glory cravers who end up knaves.

10/24/15

Wisdom at Eighteen

At eighteen I held I knew it all!
I'd recently jumped from short to tall
And was my own man none could command!
I made that known with a reprimand
To this chap n^{th} times those eighteen years;
Miserable eighteen years with my ears
Plugged and with the head of a young mule
I espoused I passed out cake and not stool
All should delight with; great colon content
Which I gave them with resolve as present.
Upon multiplying my eighteen by three
I need to follow Zacchaeus up the tree
And come down and to terms I'm not worthy
To be, by the Lamb, esteemed noteworthy.

10/24/15

By His Might

The kid in me loved climbing trees
And failed to think of Him that frees
All and keeps the twigs together;
He ventured not any farther
Than claimed all, his prowess.
Why should that kid not claim the success
When in his world arrogance veils
Mysteries confessing sight prevails
Over all unexplained knowledge?
Intubated thus there's no wedge
To stop him from diving in such
A pool in which swimmers do crush
Dreams for they are not of this world!
Yet, without dreams? Poor, poor world!

10/25/15

My Choice to Climb Down

Let them strive to climb up I'd head downward
To cling onto the greatest gift: the Word!
Their pride filled balloon shall come crashing down
And their overweighed airs would by the pound
Hit the mountain top then washed down the slope
Where with my kind we're never without rope
As the Word in His endlessness of life
Would not want to see us at odds with strife!
To lay down all at His feet for His stool
Is a choice to make needless of a school
In a world where figures not wisdom rule
Over our form of knowing with figures
As only a part jam-packed with fissures
That needs the Word to give the world treasures.

10/25/15

Why Hurry?

Till their kingdom end I'd not understand
Why people think their rush through time as grand
A design as would have wished their creator
Who in His ways hurries not to deplore
Human haste to shrink time to a shadow
After which to sprint and put up a show
With vain contention of man's importance
Before they that know no better than prance.
Breezing through time takes the mind to Divine
And exposes the treachery of landmine
Which explodes and brings forth ominous wind
Heralding deprivation of the mind
With no attention to "more haste, less speed"
With whirlwind whose cause we'd not want to plead.

10/25/15

Forget Not

While you crave a pedestal to stand on
I crave His indulgence to be reborn
To His world in which this child will always
Recall not to link Congreve's to His ways
As Congreve's ways are reputed vulgar
And would drive home grief in a popular
Wagon which fools take for their own college
Forgetting that piece on stage is collage.
Such beautiful art works have their own life
After which chimera one needs not strife
For in the shell of a mortal, accept,
We must accept to stoop low for Christ wept
Knowing we have our balloons inflated
With pride he alone could have deflated.

10/27/15

An Embrace with Failure

When failure stretched his hands I embraced him
And had the crowd bemused he got me far
For I knew there was wisdom in his jar
And if untapped I would my blessing slim

Hugo intimates from him we learn more
Where the hand of victory is just a stroke
That would caress and stoke the heart with joke
Whose clownish plight will live forevermore.

Clowns were the childhood reveries I fancied
For they always were happy from outside
Not till one old man showed me the inside
Of an egg from its shell fragranced rancid

Which perfume the haughty would with pride shield
With sham to soar above all in the field.

10/28/15

Hardened Nutshell

Fiasco thought we were friends after she'd seen
Much of me where she wished I remained green
Yet, right there I kept the profile down low
As a grain the farmer would, to make grow,
Bury underneath the earth to take root
Which roots I took and outgrew the owl's hoot;
Screeched out to give its preys a heart attack
For such targets are easy nuts to crack.
Humility does harden my nutshell
And makes sure mine is a story to tell
For every single waterhole to ooze
And thirst-quench throats on board of a cruise
Whose pride-drunk skipper flies on the topmast
Flapping his wings of disdain for my cast.

10/28-29/15

Bloom in the Tomb

Toss me in the bin
I would not fall in
Because I am down
Humble and won't drown;
Not to please foolish
Pride with his dead-wish
To see me under
Bolt struck by thunder
Of his delicate
Exotic fruit fate
Which if touched, the bloom
Is gone in the tomb
And calls for no cry
For that's when I'll fly.

10/30/15

Stainless Reflection

Beneath the stretched hand of the Almighty
With humility to His Majesty
I take shelter under the protection;
Surest I am spared of indignation
To the utter bewilderment of dupes
Whose warped thinking digs and searches for scoops
As they bury, with derision, the Truth
Which One stands against anything uncouth.
Made after keen reflection without noise,
My embrace of things divine is a choice
Left to neither chance nor coincidence
The prize of which is not in the past tense
As mine's in top form every blessed day
And gives my boundless joy free rein to play.

10/30-11/02/2015

The Stride of Pride

Long legged pride you are nothing but death!
Wickedness, your hand you stretch to bring dearth
Unto those who fancy your glitz and glam,
The trap you set for fools to shun the lamb;
An irksome ruse for all who humiliate
Themselves for His name's sake and will radiate
When they pick themselves up as ye fall down
And curse the day who robs you of the dawn;
My horseshoe moon smile will stretch to my ears
For you to hug all you thought were my fears
Then shall yours eyes be with tears unrestrained
Streaming with you screaming as if detained
In the very titivated chattel
You're garbed in and glorify as castle.

11/03-05/2015

Bamboo Life Raft

Pawn away your humility for pride
And take pride that your trade is a great stride
Mortal souls must hail with panegyrics;
Ones I loathe to the point they make me puke
Out my guts for such's the face of your book
Painting, the wise as jesters, with antics
And reveries the wind would keep you afloat
For theirs is a bamboo raft for a boat
But the wisdom of keeping the profile
Low leaves me distance to take off with style
And fly, I will fly away from foolish
Flag of ignorant arrogance you fly;
Lunacy, in the end, to make you cry
Having to embrace your ghoulish rubbish.

11/5/15

Gilded Crown of Demise

The pomp after the burial of the prince
Of arrogance should come as no surprise
To all those who've spent time paying the price
For not stooping to such a bullish lynx
The lowly all along knew they were not
And never had been jinxed with a hard nut
To crack in this bigwig whose stolen crown
Had kept him up for long then scuttled him
Down when he least projected any grim
Appeal was going to have his back down.
Royalty and humility they know
Have the potentials to make any grow;
Medicine I have taken since childhood
Needless to prove myself man in a hood.

11/06/2015

Man's Rubbisher

Man may hail pride as his furbisher
I'd tell him it is his rubbisher
He may further fly a flag of such
On a post and drink himself drunk with scotch
That glues foolishness to cowardice
With the outward apparel of vice
Which in our low estate we'd embrace
Not for we lead not our lives to race
And see whose banner flies the highest;
Though they take us for the dregs, our quest
And reserved abode are beyond the clouds
That will reduce to naught the proud crowds
Of mortals claiming this earth their kind
Quit with reproofs that drive to a bind.

11/7/15

Pride Made Outfits

To this world we come with no clue and quit
Chest thumping we had grown to vibrancy
While the ignorance of our infancy
From which our vanity hides is well lit
And had we but a little of the child
We reckon engraved with inexperience
We would need no eyes to see innocence
Does not translate the knowledge of a child
Whose eyes are not planted in the sockets
But blink as their hearts pump blood and beat
To a rhythm sweeter than sugar beet sweet
As they see adults carry their buckets
Of pride with which they make clownish outfits
And then qualify the humble misfits.

11/07-08/2015

Juvenile Humility

Could humbleness be madness;
The humble melodic sadness
Whose quiet is timidity
Or wisdom in temerity?
Humble are these children learner
Who turns their trade into earner,
Trademarked, not long before, alpha
For innocence resides not far
From wisdom who's beyond human
Understanding garbed with substance
Of self-worth moved by arrogance
That makes man a frozen saucepan
So unrepentant and blinded
To the point he's to the truth dead.

11/08/2015

Of Skunks and Pride

Filled with pride, skunks take the stench of their fart
For a fragrance that trails them in a cart
And hump their backs in an effort to burp
Not through the mouth but that orifice
That doth employ their charms to trick and tease
Those who game their lives with pride to usurp
The place of a balloon afloat in space
In hope the pie flat in its plate suffers
And embraces the fate of seafarers
Who in theirs give in to fate wielding mace
To drive ships aground and seamen to seek
The pond of mud much more the same grim creek
In Babylon by which Jews were put down
And were forced to sing a song they turned down.

11/11/2015

Lilliputian's Brobdingnagian Pride

Trade in pride and see your stride a giant's
Your triple thick skin will not court Martians
Who up above in their world take pity
In one who ought to court humility;
As mine tops my hat in form each minute
To warn against foolish pride I must quit
Or stick to it, take the heat, and rebuke
For such thrillers could not be told by Luke.
Discipleship is to take off the coat
Of disgrace in which the small minded bloat
In futile attempt to discard His grace
As they cast His design into a race
Of lesser beings good for enslavement
To which my modesty is testament.

11/11/15

Gift from the Spook

She drinks at me with color sensitive
Eyes and tags my colorlessness primitive
As her master crafts in her bloated brain
I'm worth less than that after which to game.
Yet, the flora of my humility
Makes me take spite with equanimity
Unrivalled by the joys of a blues boy king
Whose fingers softly strike the chords to bring
These sounds that keep hell sleepless night and day;
For at night when hell should be of life full
Or by day fast asleep, I do play fool
To trap that enemy who's out to play
Wise to catch fools that I refuse to be
But must give him the cruel sting of a bee.

11/11/15

Above the Fray

the sudden return home
of the town dweller made a recluse
steeped in the pride he used to abuse
and unleash on those who roam
our streets after they've gamed old country
ways in the brave name of pride
who doth ours to poetize deride
and craft a loutish dwarf tree
as home to the inane insane
they project to the height of splendor
designed in drunken stupor
for those with a tiny brain
while the dove would love perch
and let the eagle hate the dirge.

11/12/15

Long-legged Humbleness

Tall on its legs the crane
Wades across the vain
Marshland in its dole
And its tireless drinking hole
Whose effort to translate
Divine disregard, doth arrogate
Arrogance, his make believe
Panacea that would relieve
His sick psyche breaching the contract
Brokered when we came in contact
Yet, the crane's careful steps
Humble themselves to the depths
And alight with this grace
Than show up with disgrace.

11/15/15

Not for the Proud

humility's no journey for the proud
to undertake on the viewless
winged chariot of poesy
Keats and Keatsians undertake
Not to usurp loutish crafts
But one that dwells and won't vacate
The world of beauty for other finds
save one art for the world
to create, teach, and preserve
that which in the hands of nature
spells all for the world
in one simple word
that's both cake and icing
for a scrumptious crunchy gorge.

11/15/15

My World

A poem
Written
For man,
Not by
Man. Yet,
It does
Exist
And is
A bête
Noire to
The proud
Who'd not
Humble
Themselves.

11/16-17/2015

What and Where to Plant

Plant humility in hope and yield gain
If it were pride you planted, expect pain
For he holds the banner of a great fall
One that had propped emptiness to stand tall
And spite with neither terror nor favor
Which he shall know at the sign of tremor
Just when the deflated bags of meekness
Looks up to invoke the loving kindness
Rained on them from above by a Father
By whom they stay and would not stray farther
Afield to come face to face with the fate
Of the lone owls who hood for pride, their bait
Then puff and flag their plumages to show
That which they know will never ever grow.

11/19/15

Of Glut and Pride

Out of favor, struck by terror plaint not
When you stake pride and drag down all to naught
You'd smear our face with the tears of your woe

Take your folly down the valley howl then
And remind the cock to crow for the hen
To wake up to your noise thither below

Down where Dante sojourned to note treachery
The pleasures with which the damned make merry
Not a place for the likes of Lazarus

Whose veins pump not the purple colored blood
And reduce him to zilch before Dives' glut
Tyrannizing with the weight of his purse

With no notice given the mustard seed
In poor Lazarus he would one day need.

11/20/15

Treasure Slave

From my humble stance I derive pleasure
The rich does not as he slaves for treasure
Not my world atop the senses of such
Accumulators never pleased with much
But full of disdain for the peaceable
Who'd treasure a meal of vegetable
Barely acknowledged with a dash of salt
And won't, like the rich, wash it down with malt
The famed single grain grown in the Highlands
Not the Lowlands' blameless for no name brands,
Victor by landslide of popular vote,
Joy that transports me bank to bank by boat;
Yet, gives me no cause to bloat my ego
 For such street profile must be preserved low.

11/21/15

Thieving Royals

Turtle soup and venison are the choice
Princes make to leave us without a voice
Yet, my inner voice would not cease to quest
How ice cold their hearts are to nurse a rest
Without infarction and still harvest joy
And brag how they own our kind they destroy
For we hug and nurture humility
By and with whom we stand in unity
Ready to shoulder our burden with thanks
For we know our end is not one of pranks
To lure and reward us with mouths agape
Not even when their royal highnesses
See nothing wrong in robbing the masses;
For these excellent thieves, what's wrong with rape?

11/24/15

The Sparkles of Pride

The rich and powerful don't need a net
To ensnare and leave them balloon bloated
But the sparkles of pride that leaves them blind
Blind to us and to the world in a bind
Under the weight of blood thirsty warlords
To whom there is no need to keep records
Neither for the present nor the future
A practice malformed into a culture
With chants of freedom, one that swims in blood
Harvested and sold to us by their stud.
We rock the bottom of the blood river
And would live on forever and ever
As inheritors though once rejected
From the circles of the pride pageants' fete.

11/24/15

The Gloom of Meekness

The neon in city bulbs is of pride made
As the dark of our country gloom of meekness.
We country denizens by humbleness
Abide and for that reason we are paid
A recompense with thorns overloaded
Yet, expected to be seen and not heard;
How distinct are we from goats in a herd
Bound for abattoirs to be beheaded!
Equipped with a code of conduct not arms
We drop our brows at half-mast not for fear
Of man whose only acumen resides
In claims he makes of great and giant strides
Just to turn here and there and pander fear
We fear not for we know our chastening rod;
Our minder to forge ahead as we trod.

11/25/15

The Loser Wins

The rich stand agog as the Lord translates
The poor the rich cast in these base estates
For the rich swelled with pride see nothing wrong
In crushing the frail for failing to throng
And uphold and fly the flag of that mask
Of weakness worn by givers of this task
Against which the poor and frail muster strength
To take their resistance to a new length
In a fightless fight they know losers win
Leaving the rich and strong with their shared twin
Brothers, pride heralding blatant failure
Hardly perceptible from the allure
Signposted as bait for the daydreamer
Who'd push humility into coma.

11/25/15

Of Stocks and Bridges

I love stocks and bridges
Then, I heard of Stockbridge
Moved mountain and marvel
Found myself in Stockbridge
Where not stocks nor bridges
Did I find; but gravel
With her unique beauty
Drenched in humility
By splendid floral bloom
That throws greenbacks in gloom
For pride and joy they bring
Stockbridge brought to nothing
With all thronged in the street
Far from the proud Wall Street.

11/29/15

The Bait I Will not Take

As in the battle between light and darkness
Fake lights flaunt luster to highlight nothingness
Where stars need not prove they are meant to twinkle
And flag their gold hint at a periwinkle
Not as bait but one for all to take and keep
And not let it fade away but hidden deep
In the bosom of humble hearts with knowledge
The road to victory is not free of an edge
Sharpened and adorned with bait for the greedy
After earthly light deprived of eternity;
The bait none should take but rather stay away
From for it is neither life, truth, nor the way
For one to waste time and effort in pursuit
To make a point he or she can wear a suit.

11/29/15

Printed in the United States
By Bookmasters